THE
WINDOW BOX
BOOK

THE
WINDOW BOX
BOOK

by Anne Halpin
Photographs by Solomon Skolnick

Macdonald Orbis

© Running Heads Incorporated 1989

First published in Great Britain in 1989
by Macdonald & Co. (Publishers) Ltd.
London & Sydney

A member of Maxwell Pergamon Publishing Corporation plc

First published in the United States in 1989
by Simon and Schuster

The Window Box Book
was produced by
Running Heads Incorporated
42 East 23rd Street
New York, New York 10010

Senior Editor: Sarah Kirshner
Designer: Lesley Ehlers
Production Editor: Michelle Hauser

British Library Cataloguing in Publication Data

Halpin, Anne
    The window box book.
    1. Window boxes.Plants.Cultivation
    I. Title
    635.9'65

    ISBN 0-356-17890-0

Macdonald & Co (Publishers) Ltd
Headway House
66-73 Shoe Lane
London EC4P 4AB

Typeset by Nassau Typographers Inc.
Color separations by Hong Kong Scanner Craft Company, Ltd.
Printed and bound in Singapore.

CONTENTS

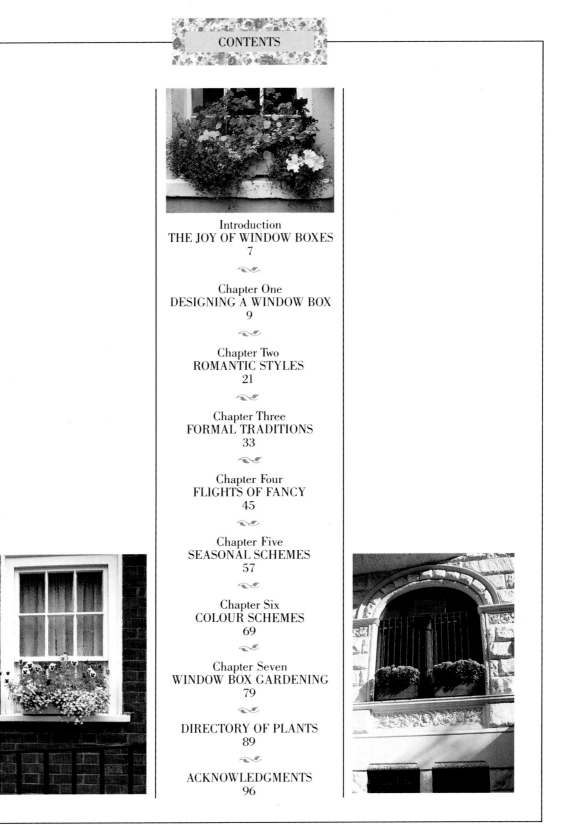

THE JOY OF WINDOW BOXES

Window boxes are an ideal way to garden. They are easy to install, simple to plant, and fun to care for. They do not require endless hours of digging, bending, and weeding to maintain. Best of all, window boxes make flowers and greenery a part of your home, growing in a place where you will see the plants often and derive continuous enjoyment from them. If you have never gardened before, planting a window box or two will enable you to try your hand at growing plants on a small and very manageable scale. If you already have a garden, or garden on a patio or rooftop, window boxes can add extra sparkle to your landscape.

This book provides an introduction to the art of gardening in window boxes. It shows you a variety of different styles and approaches: elegantly formal designs; lavish, romantic planters overflowing with delicate blossoms and flowering vines; whimsical, inventive, and unusual plantings.

Whether you live and garden in the city or country, window boxes can delight your eye and help decorate your home while demanding little of your time, money, or labour.

Left, window boxes can be mounted on railings and balconies, as well as on windowsills. Above, window boxes full of petunias (Petunia × hybrida) offer a welcoming entry to this lovely home.

CHAPTER ONE

DESIGNING A WINDOW BOX

DESIGNING A WINDOW BOX

Planning an effective window box involves many of the same design considerations as planning a garden bed or border, although in far simpler form. To get maximum visual impact you need to consider the site, environment, and type of plants you desire, just as you do when you plan a garden bed.

An understanding of a few basic principles of garden design will enable you to create sumptuously beautiful window boxes that are perfectly suited to their environment.

EVALUATING THE WINDOW BOX SITE

With any garden site, you must consider both climate (the average weather in the region where you live) and microclimate (the local environmental conditions that exist on your property, or in this case, your windowsill). The first steps in designing your window boxes are deciding where you want to put them and evaluating the conditions present there.

An awareness of the limiting factors imposed by the environment on your windowsills will help guide your plant selections. For example, if you live where winters are severe you will need to choose plants that can withstand the lowest winter temperatures in

Left, cascading ivy-leaved geraniums (Pelargonium peltatum) *and variegated ivy* (Hedera helix) *soften the sharp lines of the windows and French doors of this townhouse. Above, a tiny terracotta planter holds a sprightly mix of Shasta daisies* (Chrysanthemum maximum), *yellow pansies* (Viola × wittrockiana), *purple lobelia and a rosy pink* Pelargonium peltatum.

Above, window boxes of red pelargoniums and white petunias
(Petunia × hybrida) *strike a
festive note on this front porch .
A hanging basket of fuchsias*
(Fuchsia × hybrida) *and a glossy
green* schefflera *spending the
summer outdoors complete the
garden .* *Right*, *informal window
boxes of geraniums and petunias
add charm to this rustic barn .*

Above, trailing ivy (Hedera helix) *grows with petunias and a* coleus. *Below*, *cascading lobelia* (Lobelia erinus) *blends with impatiens in rosy red, pink, and white. Red pelargoniums add height.*

your area. You may also need to provide protection for shrubs and perennials left outdoors in winter. On the other hand, if you live in a warmer climate, you will be able to leave tender perennials outside, such as pelargoniums and fuchsias during the winter. Window boxes, because they hold so little soil, dry out more quickly than garden beds, so it is especially important to choose plants that don't need much water for window boxes unless you're prepared to water them regularly.

It is important to be aware of the amount of sunlight your window boxes will receive. Sun and shadow patterns shift during the course of the day and from season to season. A window box may get four or five hours of direct morning or afternoon sun in summer, but no direct light at all in winter, when the sun is lower in the sky.

If your window boxes will be in shade part of the day, you will enjoy the greatest success with plants that either tolerate or prefer such conditions. Impatiens, wax begonias, hostas, bulbs, or ferns are ideal for shady spots.

Wind is another important consideration. If your boxes will be located on the side of the house or building which faces into the prevailing winds, concentrate on growing compact, sturdy plants. In very windy locations, you may need to provide stakes or other supports for all your plants. Urban flat dwellers should think carefully about wind. Tall buildings in cities create strong winds that change speed and direction quickly and often, winds that can tear delicate flowers and leaves off their stems, leaving plants looking ragged and battered.

If you live in a large city you should pay attention to the quality of the air to which your plants are exposed. Many plants, particularly delicate ones, do not grow well in polluted air. Check the *Directory of Plants*, page 89, for appropriate plants for your particular needs.

SEASONAL INTEREST AND COLOUR SCHEMES

Most window boxes are primarily summertime gardens, but you can also plan them to provide colour in spring or autumn, or even winter in mild climates. The key to success is to plan in advance and choose plants carefully. If you want your window boxes to bloom in spring, in summer, and in autumn, you can grow seasonal plants in individual pots or in plastic liners that you slip into the window boxes when the plants are ready to come into bloom.

One of the most enjoyable parts of planning a window garden is choosing the colours of the flowers and foliage you want to have in your box. Many different colour schemes are possible in window boxes, and because window gardens are small, it is easy to experiment with different colours from season to season and year to year.

WORKING WITH PLANT FORMS AND SIZES

Although most window boxes are more or less rectangular in shape, window box gardens should not

Above, a cleverly integrated window box combines trailing ivy (Hedera helix) with ivy-leaved geraniums (Pelargonium pel-tatum) and white daisies. Below, deep green foliage beautifully sets off blossoms in rich red and sparkling white.

Above, in this informal window box, unpruned box (Buxus sempervirens) *adds height, white pansies* (Viola × wittrockiana) *add mass, and ivy* (Hedera helix) *trails over the front of the planter to soften its harsh edge. Right, this side view shows how varying plant heights from front to back provides depth and fullness to a window box.*

look flat and two-dimensional. Just like a well-planned garden, these gardens-in-miniature are more interesting when they have depth and variation of plant heights.

A row of plants all the same height looks boring and unnatural. In nature plants are not all the same height. Using plants of varying heights will give your window boxes a more naturalistic look. For the best results, plant taller plants in the back of the box, shorter plants in the middle, and low edging or trailing plants in the front of the box to balance the tall plants in the back. Allow trailers to spill over

Above, impatiens blooms lavishly in shady spots, and provides masses of colour in places too dim for many other plants to flower.

the front of the box to give the box an air of exuberance and charm. Edging or cascading plants and flowers also give the window box a softer, less contrived look. Climbing vines planted at the back of a window box can add extra height to a window garden. Support them on a small trellis to one side of the box, or train them to grow up and around the window to frame the view from indoors.

When planting the boxes, do not line up your three sizes of plants in straight rows like little soldiers. For a more flowing, natural look, stagger the plants in the rows, placing some a bit farther back and others slightly forward.

You can also use plant heights to create movement in the window box design. To bring movement to a planting, vary the plant heights from side to side across the box as well as from front to back. You can create a strong, angular direction or a soft curve, depending on how you position the plants.

Finally, take into account the size and shape of the window where the box will be positioned, and keep the plants in scale with the window. Small windows look best with small plants; tall, narrow windows can accommodate taller plants, although the plants should not be so tall that they completely block the windows. If the window is very narrow, consider planting one or two tall plants at one end of the box, and grading to shorter plants at the opposite end of the box. Vines and climbing plants are also particularly attractive when trained around tall, narrow windows.

INDOOR/OUTDOOR WINDOW BOXES

Many houseplants enjoy spending summer outdoors, and a window box makes a good summer home for small and medium-size plants.

A window box planted entirely with houseplants or tropical species can go outdoors for the summer and come back inside in early autumn, before the weather turns cold. If you want to put some houseplants in a window box along with annuals or other outdoor plants, it is easiest to leave the houseplants in their pots and set them into the window box.

Below, coleus is an outstanding plant to grow in partial shade. Its beautifully variegated leaves come in a whole range of shapes, sizes, and colours.

CHAPTER TWO

ROMANTIC
STYLES

Left, a romantic assortment of flowers in mixed colours inspired by English cottage gardens. Roses planted under the windows complement these window boxes of nasturtiums (Tropaeolum *species),* lobelia, marigolds (Tagetes patula), *and other flowers.* Below, *Swedish ivy* (Plectranthus) *tumbles over the front of this sun-washed window box full of annuals.*

ROMANTIC STYLES

There is no specific criterion that defines what is meant by a romantic window box, but many window boxes do create a decidedly romantic impression. Romance is a quality — a general feeling — imparted by the plants, the containers, and the setting. The overall impression is one of lushness, delicacy, and sensuality. Romantic window boxes appeal to the senses rather than the intellect. They delight the eye with a profusion of greenery of varying shapes and sizes, and flowers in soft pastel shades or a mix of bright, lively colours. Fragrant flowers are ideal for romantic boxes. You can also plant foliage and blossoms of varying textures to appeal to the sense of touch.

Romantic window boxes are not about straight lines and sharp angles. Instead, these plantings are full of soft curves and natural, irregular shapes. Diagonal stems and branches add movement and life to the design. The most romantic-looking window boxes are lush with plants allowed to tumble together in playful disorder, like a somewhat overgrown garden. Trailers and ground covers such as periwinkle (*Vinca minor)* and ivy (*Hedera helix*

Below, the tiniest imaginable planter holds just two lobelia plants, one sweet alyssum (Lobularia maritima), and a single wax begonia (Begonia × semperflorens-cultorum), whose colours gleam like jewels in a niche in a plain brick wall.

species) spill over the edges of the container. Flowering vines entwine as they climb the wall or windowframe above the box. Inside the container, delicate foliage and old-fashioned flowers intermingle their colours and scents in cheerful abandon.

Plant forms in a romantic window box tend to be delicate. A romantic garden does not look sleek or contemporary, but instead conveys a sense of gentleness and nostalgia. This is not the place for bold, sculptural plants like yuccas or bromeliads, which

make dramatic statements. It is also not the place for meticulously pruned shrubs and conifers, or for topiary or plants trained as standards. To achieve a romantic look, allow the plants to assume, as much as space will permit, their natural shapes and growing habits. Basic maintenance like picking off spent flowers is important, but leave precise pruning for formal gardens.

One particularly evocative way to create a feeling of romance is to echo aspects of traditional English cottage gardens. Obviously you cannot have a true

Above, lavishly flowering lobelia, pelargonium, and petunia spill over the edges of this charming window box. A gold-spotted aucuba adds height in the rear.

Below, ivy-leaved geraniums (Pelargonium peltatum) are lovely against the decorative wrought iron grille in the front of this window. Right, English ivy (Hedera helix) clambers around the stone lintel of this city townhouse. Cheerful marigolds (Tagetes patula) and geraniums (Pelargonium × hortorum) add splashes of warm colour.

cottage garden in a window box. But you can adapt some of the features — old-fashioned flowers, mixed colour schemes — to create a look reminiscent of a cottage garden, a gentle reminder of days gone by.

Old-fashioned flowers to consider for window boxes include spicy-scented garden pinks (*Dianthus* species), sweet William (*Dianthus barbatus*), heartsease (*Viola tricolour*), pansies (*Viola × wittrockiana*), violets (*Viola odorata*), fuchsia (*Fuchsia* cultivars), candytuft (*Iberis* species), cornflower or bachelor's button (*Centaurea cyanus*), tobacco plant (*Nicotiana alata*), nasturtium (*Tropaeolum minus* or *T. majus*, the climbing type), feverfew (*Chrysanthemum parthenium*), pot marigold (*Calendula officinalis*), the fragrant wallflower (*Cheiranthus cheiri*), wild primrose (*Primula vulgaris*), French marigold (*Tagetes patula*), Iceland poppy (*Papaver nudicaule*), and Shirley poppy (*Papaver Rhoeas*). Roses are another traditional cottage garden plant, and if they appeal to you, you can grow one of the miniature varieties.

Flowering vines to try for a romantic effect include morning glory (*Ipomoea purpurea*), the closely related night-blooming moonflower (*Ipomoea alba*), exotic passionflowers (*Passiflora* species), sweet-scented honeysuckles (*Lonicera* species) and jasmines (*Jasminum* species), black-eyed Susan (*Thunbergia alata*), canary creeper (*Tropaeolum peregrinum*), and sweet peas (*Lathyrus odorata*), with their intense, spicy-sweet fragrance.

<u>*Above*</u>, *this romantic little garden combines different plants in a casually random arrangement of containers. Dwarf dahlias* (Dahlia *species) grace the window box, red wax begonias* (Begonia × semperflorens-cultorum) *grow in tiny pots on the wall and plant stand, and fragrant sweet peas* (Lathyrus odorata) *dangle from the hanging basket on the left. Lavender* (Lavandula angustifolia) *grows in the pot directly below.*

<u>*Right*</u>, *a lush, two-tiered window box turns this shopfront into a cool, green garden oasis.*

Left, a long window box full of summer flowers keeps company with a climbing rose, while honeysuckle festoons the railing. *Below*, a fragrant wisteria (twined about the iron railing) finishes blooming and turns the show over to a window box full of pink pelargoniums in this lovely city entrance garden. The carefully pruned holly tree in the tub adds a note of formality to this otherwise romantic scene.

CHAPTER THREE

FORMAL TRADITIONS

FORMAL TRADITIONS

Formal gardens are concerned with abstract principles of symmetry, balance, proportion, and line. They are designed on strong, straight vertical and horizontal axes. Straight lines and sharp angles define the plantings, creating a feeling of stability and stillness. Diagonals, which create movement, are not found in these gardens. All the elements of the garden are in scale with one another.

Plants in formal gardens are pruned into idealized shapes — upright evergreens are clipped into cones or pyramids, hedges are straight with precisely squared sides, elaborate flower beds are enclosed with walls or low hedges called parterres. Topiaries are also part of many formal gardens — plants are meticulously trained to assume the shapes of animals, objects, or geometric figures. Not a twig, not a leaf is permitted out of place in a formal garden.

To those of us who love the infinite variety of natural plant forms and who enjoy watching plants grow and flourish, formal gardens often seem cold and overly mannered. But for all their artifice, formal gardens are stately and serene, and formal

Left, a symmetrical planting of lavender lobelia, pink impatiens, and red pelargonium surrounds a small false cypress (Chamaecyparis). Above, white pansies (Viola × wittrockiana) against a background of evergreens make a serene and restful box.

Left, a simple colour scheme and carefully maintained plants create an elegant entrance garden of shrubs and flowers. _Above_, upright, neatly clipped evergreens give the planting harmony and stability.

planting styles nicely complement the architecture of many homes.

The same qualities found in formal gardens can be achieved on a miniature scale in window boxes. Formal window boxes are best suited to period homes and buildings, particularly in urban areas.

To achieve the necessary feeling of repose, a formal window box needs balance and stability. Design the window box on a strong horizontal axis punctuated with equally strong verticals. Avoid diagonals that would create a feeling of movement, and flowing curves that would encourage the viewer's eye to move from one part of the planting to another when observing the box.

You might start with a small evergreen in the centre rear of the window box, or perhaps a row of three small trees in a larger box to provide a vertical focal point. The trees should be pruned into neat,

Above, containers of chrysanthemum of the same height create an elegant autumn garden. Right, symmetry is an important part of achieving a formal look. In this window box, evergreens are punctuated with pelargoniums of similar size and shape, with lobelia in the front of the box and ivy trailing over the sides.

perfect shapes. If you want a formal look without using trees or shrubs, you can design a symmetrical planting of flowers and foliage plants. Some variation of plant heights is important to add interest to the design, but try to keep the design simple and orderly. Concentrate on placing taller plants in the back of the box and shorter plants in front.

Formal window boxes require scrupulous maintenance to have them look their best at all times. If plants become overgrown, the elegant lines and forms disappear, and the planting looks unkempt.

Above, the trailing ivy is kept carefully in bounds here, and it is balanced by a lobelia on either side.

Above, the symmetry of these containers of wax begonias (Begonia × semperflorens-cultorum) *and sweet alyssum* (Lobularia maritima) *has a cool, formal appearance. Below, although not strictly formal, this carefully composed planting of pelargoniums, ivy, and daisies makes a classic circular shape.*

Containers for formal window gardens can be either sleekly elegant (fibreglass, for example, or wood painted white or a dark neutral colour) or an antique style (such as a stone or concrete trough with a classical motif).

Dwarf evergreens are the plants most often used for vertical accents in formal window boxes. Good candidates include dwarf cultivars of box (*Buxus sempervirens*), false cypress (*Chamaecyparis* species), juniper (*Juniperus* species), bay (*Laurus nobilis*) in mild climates, and for large boxes, hollies (*Ilex* species). Some gardeners like to grow plants trained as standards — neat balls of foliage atop straight, bare

stems. Box (*Rosmarinus* species) is one possibility although it must be pruned regularly to keep its shape. Geraniums (*Pelargonium* varieties) and chrysanthemums (*Chrysanthemum* × *morifolium*) can also be trained as standards.

Many kinds of flowers can work in formal window boxes, but the best choices are plants with neat growing habits. Upright plants such as geraniums, tulips (*Tulipa* species and hybrids), and daffodils and narcissus (*Narcissus* species and hybrids) work well, as do plants that form compact mounds, like impatiens (*Impatiens* species).

Above, this garden looks formal even though it contains several colours, because the plants are meticulously groomed and arranged in parallel patterns.

This window box is something of a hybrid between romantic and formal styles. The colours and soft shapes are romantic, but the symmetry of the plants and the neat, precise maintenance bring a feeling of calm control to the garden. The tall bay trees on either side help anchor and stabilize the more active plants in the box.

CHAPTER FOUR

FLIGHTS
OF FANCY

FLIGHTS OF FANCY

This chapter presents an assortment of unusual, innovative, and interesting approaches to window box gardens. Perhaps it will inspire you to try out some creative ideas of your own.

You might decide to add some houseplants to window boxes of summer flowers or, if you live in a warm, humid climate, to grow cool green foliage plants. If summers are hot and dry in your part of the world, you could fill your window boxes with cacti and succulents. You might combine annual and perennial flowers, or add a small sculpture or garden ornament to the scene. If you haven't space for a conventional kitchen garden, window boxes can allow you to grow some food plants. If your ideal is living in a plant-filled secret bower, you can make your garden dream come true by combining window boxes with pots, hanging baskets, and trellises.

FOLIAGE PLANTS

Lush, bold-leaved foliage plants can turn an ordinary window box into a cool oasis. You can combine foliage of different shapes, sizes, and textures, varying shades of green, and assorted patterns and colours. Many tropical plants are popular houseplants,

Left, this fanciful planting combines a bold-leaved Fatsia japonica, *which is often grown as a houseplant, with tiny-leaved ivies and evergreens in various shades of green. Purple lobelia and red and pink fuchsia add colour. Above, glossy foliage in several shades of green is beautifully set off by green-and-white ivies and colourful annuals in a jungle-like garden.*

A whimsical assortment of foliage and flowers in pots, window boxes, and hanging baskets has turned this outdoor cafe into an enchanting green bower.

and they can perform just as beautifully outdoors when the weather is warm. Consider Chinese evergreens (*Aglaonema* species) with leaves of solid green or green and white, or *Fatsia japonica*, with its large palmate leaves. *Spathiphyllum* and young specimens of *Dieffenbachia* are other good choices.

Variegated foliage is particularly interesting, and there are many plants with patterned and coloured leaves. When you are searching through books and catalogues for these plants, keep in mind that the words *picta*, *marginata*, and *variegata* in plants' botanical names are all clues to foliage that is streaked, striped, splashed, or splotched with white or other colours. The polka dot plant (*Hypoestes phyllostachya*) has pink dots all over its green leaves. Spotted laurel (*Aucuba japonica*) is spotted and splashed with golden yellow. The leaves of the ti plant (*Cordyline terminalis*) are edged and striped

Above, in autumn the now-leafless vine clinging to its tiny trellis looks like a piece of sculpture. *Right*, daisies in the midst of the city bring a reminder of open meadows.

with bright pink. *Dracaena marginata* has deep green sword-shaped leaves with red edges. *Coleus* species and hybrids come in a wide variety of colours and patterns in combinations of deep green, lime green, red, pink, and white. Crotons (*Codiaeum pictum*) can combine deep red, bright orange-red, golden yellow, and green.

Foliage is more than just a green backdrop for flowers. It can be fascinating in itself, and there are endless variations for creative gardeners to explore.

EDIBLES

Garden-fresh herbs and vegetables are two of the great delights of the kitchen, and many edibles grow

Above, an innovative planting of hollyhocks, annuals, and a Shasta daisy (Chrysanthemum maximum) trained into a tree shape join with an elegant piece of sculpture to welcome visitors to a small art gallery.

This portable garden travels with its owners on a charmingly painted vacation houseboat.

Right, variegated leaves on the vine stems twist off into space in many directions, giving this window box a decidedly playful air. Below, kitchen herbs bask in the late-summer sun outside this city window.

quite happily in the confines of a window box. Tall herbs to grow in the back of a window box include feathery dill (*Peucedanum graveolens*), borage (*Borago officinalis*), and fennel (*Foeniculum vulgare*). Basil is another good choice for pots and window boxes. In addition to the classic sweet basil (*Ocimium basilicum*), there are varieties with small leaves, purple leaves, and scents of lemon, cinnamon, or licorice. Chives (*Allium schoenoprasum*) have round, purple-pink flower heads in summer, and there are giant varieties as well as the ordinary species.

Other herbs to consider for window boxes include sweet marjoram (*Origanum majorana*), oregano (*Origanum vulgare*), curly or fern-leaved parsley (*Petroselinum crispum*), balm (*Melissa officinalis*), and sage (*Salvia officinalis*).

Left, *this summer window box combines pink-flowered Madagascar periwinkle* (catharanthus roseus) *with Asparagus ferns and spider plants* (Chlorophytum *species) from the indoor garden. The tiny pink flowers of heather* (Erica) *add pinpoints of colour. Below, striped petunias turn a windowbox into a fanciful collection of pinwheels.*

Thyme (*Thymus vulgaris*) is a good plant for the front of a window box, and its tiny leaves can be green, variegated with gold, or lemon-scented, depending on the variety.

Window boxes can provide you with a small harvest of vegetables, too. Peas or pole beans can be trained up a trellis in the back of the box. Salad greens and miniature varieties of other favourite crops will grow in window boxes, too. If lettuce is your fancy, consider a compact romaine or cos variety called Little Gem, butterheads Tom Thumb or All the Year Round, or loose-leaf types like Salad Bowl, Red Salad Bowl, Red Sails, or Oak Leaf. Sophisticated salad lovers will want to try lamb's lettuce, sorrel, garden cress, or radicchio.

You could also grow radishes or small varieties of beets, carrots, aubergine or eggplant, and tomatoes.

CHAPTER FIVE

SEASONAL
SCHEMES

SEASONAL SCHEMES

Left, pansies start blooming in spring and flower best in cool weather. They are joined here by masses of white lobelia. *Below*, late spring pansies and violas keep company with the first of the summer pelargoniums.

Like conventional gardens, window boxes can be planned to provide interest over successive seasons, or to put on a big display at a particular time of year. You can plan window box gardens to reach their peak in spring, summer, autumn, or all three. If you live in a warm climate where winters are mild, your window boxes can be full of plants in winter as well.

Planning for successions of flowers in window boxes is actually easier than planning a garden bed or border, because window boxes are too small to hold all the plants at once. To plant seasonal window boxes, you will have to plant each season's flowers in separate boxes, pots, or liners, and re-place one season's plants with the next. While this means you will have to find places other than your windowsills for plants out of season, you will have the advantage of being able to plan each season's display without regard to the plants that were in your window boxes the season before, or what will follow next season.

SPRING

Where winters are cold, spring is the most welcome time of year, especially for gardeners. Few moments

Above, as spring turns to summer, yellow violas bloom with red petunias on a sunny windowsill. The deep pink flowers are the first to open on two regal pelarganiums (Pelargonium × domesticum).

are as rewarding to gardeners as the sight of the first green shoots pushing their way through the surface of the cold earth, whether that earth is in a garden bed or a window box.

The first flowers to bloom in spring belong to hardy bulbs, and many of these bulbs grow quite happily in window boxes. The possibilities include *Crocus*, daffodils and narcissus (*Narcissus* species), rich blue *Scilla siberica* and glory-of-the-snow (*Chionodoxa* species), fragrant hyacinths (*Hyacinthus orientalis*), and the shorter-stemmed tulips (*Tulipa* species), especially the Greigii and Kauf-

manniana or waterlily hybrids. When the plants become crowded after a few years, lift, divide, and
replant the bulbs to give them more space.

Bulbs are not the only spring flowers that will
bloom in window boxes. There are perennials such
as white-flowered candytuft (*Iberis sempervirens*);
rock cress (*Arabis* species), which blooms in white
or pink; *Aubrieta* species, with flowers of pink or
purple; the aptly named gold dust (*Aurinia saxatilis*); horned violets (*Viola cornuta*), in golden orange, cream, or purple; and polyanthus primroses

Below, this purple lobelia began
blooming in spring and will continue all summer long if flowers
are picked off as they fade.

Above, petunias (Petunia × hybrida) *and geraniums (Pelargonium × hortorum) in red and white bloom all summer long on this sunny windowsill. Right, petunias, geraniums, and lobelia in harmonious shades of pink and purple put on a lavish show in summer.*

This summer garden combines upright purple lobelia with deep red fuchsia, rose-pink pelargonium, aucuba, and trailing ivy (Hedera helix).

Impatiens are classic summer plants for shady locations.

(*Primula* × *polyantha*) in their many shades of red, rose, pink, purple, blue, yellow, and white.

Veronica species and perennial garden pinks (*Dianthus* species) also start blooming in spring.

Hardy annuals and biennials also begin to bloom in spring, before the heat of summer sets in. Pansies (*Viola* × *wittrockiana*), which come in many shades of yellow, gold, orange, purple, blue and white, either with or without distinctive face-like markings, bloom beautifully in cool spring weather and work wonderfully in window boxes. You can buy plants at a local garden centre if you prefer not to bother starting seeds yourself. Other good choices are cornflower or bachelor's button (*Centaurea cyanus*), calendula or pot marigold (*Calendula officinalis*), love-in-a-mist (*Nigella damascena*), Virginia stocks (*Malcomia maritima*), and climbing sweet peas, which also bring the bonus of their heavenly fragrance.

SUMMER

Summer is prime time for annuals, and besides the ubiquitous geraniums (*Pelargonium* species), petunias (*Petunia* × *hybrida*), impatiens (*Impatiens* species), and French marigolds (*Tagetes patula*), there are many other summer-blooming annuals to choose from, as well as biennials and perennials that will bloom in the first year.

Blue and purple flowers include flossflower (*Ageratum houstonianum*); *Browallia speciosa*; cup

flower (*Nierembergia hippomanica*); dwarf varieties of *Phlox drummondii*; the very popular *Lobelia erinus*, which can also be had in red or white; globe candytuft (*Iberis umbellata*); and mealycup sage (*Salvia farinacea*). A pretty plant for a shady box is the wishbone flower, *Torenia Fournieri*.

Red, rose, and pink summer flowers include snapdragons (*Antirrhinum majus*), pyrethrum or painted daisy (*Chrysanthemum coccineum*), *Verbena* species, *Cosmos*, China asters (*Callistephus chinensis*), wax begonia (*Begonia* × *semperfloren-scultorum*), zinnias (*Zinnia elegans*), *Fuchsia*, tobacco plant (*Nicotiana* species), creeping Madagascar periwinkle (*Catharanthus roseus*), field poppies (*Papaver rhoeas*), and globe amaranth (*Gomphrena globosa*). In hot, dry locations, try growing the daisy-like flowers of ice plant (*Mesembryanthemum crystallinum*) or the brilliantly coloured and low-growing sun plant (*Portulaca grandiflora*).

If you want yellow and orange flowers, consider nasturtiums (*Tropaeolum majus* or *T. minus*), the climbing canary creeper (*Tropaeolum peregrinum*), *Coreopsis*, *Celosia*, African daisy (*Arctotis stoechadifolia*), cape marigold (*Dimorphotheca* species), and calendulas.

White summer flowers include honey-scented sweet alyssum (*Lobularia maritima*), which also comes in pink, lilac, and purple; Shasta daisies (*Chrysanthemum maximum*); and white varieties of *Petunia*, *Begonia*, *Pelargonium*, and *Impatiens*.

Petunias and geraniums in red and white are good summer flowers for sunny window boxes.

This summer planting combines euonymus, lobelia, pelargonium, and an evergreen.

Above, chrysanthemums are autumn classics in gardens and windowboxes. Below, many annuals keep blooming until the first autumn frost including petunias (Petunia × hybrida), *scarlet sage* (Salvia splendens), *marigolds* (Tagetes patula), *and ageratum.*

Some summer tubers that are suitable for window boxes are tuberous begonia (*Begonia* × *tuberhydrida*), whose showy double flowers light up a shady spot with warm, rich reds, yellows, oranges, and pinks; and dwarf cultivars of *Dahlia*, which bloom from late summer well into autumn, depending upon the variety.

AUTUMN

The classic autumn flower is, of course, the hardy chrysanthemum (*Chrysanthemum* × *morifolium*), whose warm-toned flowers echo the colours of autumn foliage. In addition, you can choose 'mums' with purple, white, or pink flowers. The best

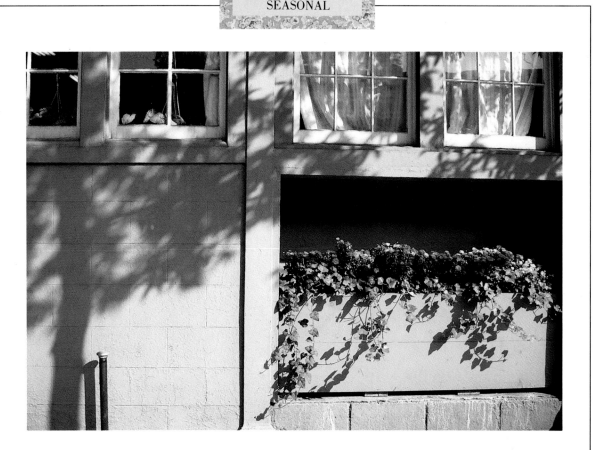

chrysanthemums for window boxes are compact varieties such as cushion, pompon, or button mums.
Because the plants are quite demanding and do not
grow well for everyone, you may find it easiest to
buy new plants for your window boxes each autumn
rather than trying to overwinter them.

If chrysanthemums do not hold great appeal for
you but you still want autumnal flowers, try planting
autumn bulbs — autumn crocus and colchicum
(whose flowers resemble large crocuses). These
bulbs are planted in summer to bloom in a matter of
weeks. The colour range is like that of spring
crocuses.

*Above, dainty pink chrysan-
themums team up with ivy in this
graceful, pastel-coloured autumnal garden. Below, warm, copp-
ery chrysanthemums are
beautiful against the cool grey
stone of this block of flats.*

CHAPTER SIX

COLOUR SCHEMES

COLOUR SCHEMES

To achieve the best visual effect with window boxes, it is important to give some thought to the colours you will use in them. Many kinds of colour schemes are possible, from soft combinations of pastels to contrasting bold, bright hues. Combining colours in window boxes is much the same as combining them in garden beds. However, because you will be working with a limited number of plants in a small space, the most successful colour schemes for window boxes are generally simple ones. There are several basic approaches you can take when mixing colours in your window boxes.

MONOCHROMATIC SCHEMES

Monochromatic schemes — the simplest kind — combine flowers of a single colour, or shades of a single colour, with the green of foliage and stems. For example, you might opt for an all-yellow garden, or all red, or white. You can add white to a basic monochromatic garden to brighten and add sparkle to the overall look. Window boxes in monochromatic schemes, with or without the addition of white, tend to be calm and serene, and lend themselves to formal planting styles.

Left, summer annuals in a riot of colours create a cheerful garden. The window box and other pots contain petunias (Petunia ×hybrida), geraniums (Pelargonium ×hortorum), lobelia (Lobelia erinus), marigolds (Tagetes patula), fuchsias (Fuchsia hybrida) and nasturtiums (Tropaeolum species). Tucked into the back of the window box is a white snapdragon (Antirrhinum majus). Above, this window box full of sun-loving petunias and geraniums (pelargoniums) shows a well-planned mix of plant heights, and nice depth.

Left, in this monochromatic window box, the bright rose-pink of the petunias works beautifully with their green leaves and the neutral tones of the surrounding stonework. Right, another successful monochromatic garden mixes geraniums in two warm shades of pink with foliage in various shades of green.

Below, bright golden chrysanthemums brighten an otherwise somber combination of deep green hedge and grey-blue woodwork.

ANALOGOUS SCHEMES

Analogous or related colour schemes blend colours that are close to one another on an artist's colour wheel, and therefore, harmonize beautifully. Pink and purple is one analogous combination; red, orange, and yellow is another. Pastels usually work beautifully in analogous colour schemes. White flowers or silver foliage can be added to lighten and brighten the effect.

CONTRASTING SCHEMES

Complementary or contrasting colour schemes are a riskier but interesting approach to mixing hues. Complementary colours are opposite one another on the colour wheel. Red and green are complementary, as are blue and orange, and purple and yellow. When a colour is placed next to its complement, the effect is to make both colours appear stronger. Such extreme contrasts can easily become jarring in a

Below, pinks and purples create wonderful colour harmonies in the garden. This window box blends pink and deep purple petunias (Petunia × hybrida) *with lobelia in a lighter purple.*

garden, especially in a small window box. But when sensitively handled, contrasting colour schemes can be lively and fun. The key to success is to choose carefully among the shades and tints of the two colours to find combinations that do not fight each other. You can also use colours that are contrasting without being exactly complementary.

POLYCHROMATIC SCHEMES

Polychromatic or mixed colour schemes follow no rules — the choice of colours is strictly up to the whim of the gardener. The cheerful riot of colours found in traditional cottage gardens exemplifies the polychromatic approach.

While mixed colour schemes can be lots of fun, they can also easily become chaotic, especially within the confines of a window box. Whatever colour scheme you use, consider how the colours will work with the colour and the architectural style of your home. Think about the texture of the wall as well as the colour of the window frames and doors. If the wall is a dark colour, or receives shade for much of the day, use pastels or white-flowered plants in your window boxes. If your wall is white or cream-coloured, use bright pastels or rich, strong colours. If your window box will receive lots of sun, bright, strong colours will work best.

Above, a softer combination in the same colour family mixes lobelia from deep purple to palest lavender with impatiens in rose-pink and light pink, and fuchsia in soft pink and white.

Left, the bold combination of colours on this window ledge is a dramatic polychromatic scheme. Pastel colours would be lost against the neutral wall in such fierce sunlight. *Above*, one key to success in multicoloured window boxes is to choose related colours and surround them with lots of green. The yellow pansies in this garden contain tinges of red that relate very well to the red lobelia and impatiens.

CHAPTER SEVEN

WINDOW BOX GARDENING

WINDOW BOX GARDENING

~

Gardening in window boxes is quite different from gardening in beds and borders. You will be able to exercise more control over the soil mix in which the plants grow. Plants in window boxes need to be watered and fertilized more frequently than plants in garden beds, because the volume of soil is so much smaller. It dries out rapidly and its nutrients become exhausted quickly. This chapter provides basic instructions on how to garden in window boxes.

CONTAINERS

Window boxes are all the same basic rectangular shape — long and narrow — but they are available in a variety of styles, materials, and colours. They can be simple or fancy, and be made of wood, metal, stone, fibreglass or clay.

A window box that will sit directly on the windowsill should be a few centimetres (inches) shorter than the width of the sill so that you can get your hands around the ends of the box when you lift it on and off the sill. If you will be mounting the box on the wall below the windowsill, the length is not as critical. The window box can be a bit wider than the windowsill and supported with brackets screwed or

Left a delightful union of window box gardening with a creative outdoor landscape.

bolted into the wall.

When choosing a container for your window box, get the deepest one you can find. It should be at least 15 cm (6 in) deep — 30 cm (12 in) is even better, if your window is large enough to accommodate it. The deeper the box, the more space is available for plant roots, and the wider your choice of plants. Also, since a deeper box holds more soil, the box will not dry out as rapidly as a very shallow box, and you will not have to water the plants quite as often.

Simple containers are the most versatile. A plain container blends in with most architectural styles, and does not detract attention from the plants growing inside it. Neutral colours — grey, beige, brown, natural wood — are easiest to work with, because they do not detract from the colours of the building or the plants. Window boxes are also available in white (which will need frequent cleaning, especially in dirty city air) or green. You can also paint the boxes to match the trim on your house. If you plan to mount the boxes on the wall below the windowsills, you may want to paint them the same colour as the wall. Also keep in mind that flat matt paint does not stand out as much as glossy paint, and is probably a better choice.

A stained wooden box raised on blocks to allow drainage.

A textured window box of neutral-coloured concrete.

An antique stone trough suits the mood of this elegant urban townhouse.

You can choose from a number of different materials when selecting window boxes. One of the best is fibreglass. Fibreglass boxes are durable, hold up well in both hot and cold weather, and are relatively inexpensive. One sleek model sold by numerous mail-order garden supply companies looks like white-painted wood. Fibreglass boxes are also easy to clean — a real plus.

Plastic boxes are light in weight and easy to handle, and they retain moisture well. If you opt for plastic boxes, make sure they are made of a durable, heavyweight plastic; cheap, thin plastic boxes become brittle after spending time in the sunlight, and tend to crack and break.

Wood is the classic material for window boxes. You can buy ready-made boxes or build your own, if you are so inclined. The natural look of stained or varnished wood is ideal for country houses and summer or weekend homes. Painted wood boxes can look sophisticated enough for a contemporary or city home. Wood is a good insulator, and protects plant roots from extreme temperatures better than plastic, clay, or metal boxes. Teak and redwood make especially durable containers. To prolong the life of wood window boxes, it is best to coat the inside with a wood preservative that is nontoxic to plants, or plant in removable plastic liners that slip inside the boxes.

Metal containers are less desirable because they rust quickly and are good conductors of heat and cold, and therefore do little to insulate plant roots from fluctuating temperatures. If you do choose metal boxes, make sure they are well painted or coated with plastic or polyurethane to make them last as long as possible.

Terracotta window boxes are attractive and natural-looking and their neutral colour complements many flower colours. Unglazed clay or terracotta window boxes are porous and allow moisture to transpire quickly through their sides. They also break easily, especially in cold weather. (Freezing temperatures often crack them.)

Stone and concrete troughs can also be used as window boxes. These troughs usually carry ornate patterns, many of them copied from antique pieces. These containers are most appropriate for historic and period houses, since their look is usually not contemporary. They are fairly expensive, and very heavy to move about, but they are quite stately and handsome.

An unusual window box option is to use oblong wire

A gaily painted wooden box makes a cheerful, individual gardening statement.

A box of unfinished wood looks just right against this rough wood siding.

Fibreglass boxes are versatile and do not call attention to themselves; the plants are the stars of this garden.

baskets which at least one supplier calls "hayracks." Before planting, line the baskets with overlapping pieces of moistened sphagnum moss to hold the soil mix. These baskets are not as convenient to use as other window boxes, and they dry out even more quickly.

Window boxes are available in garden centres, and in shops located in botanic gardens and other public gardens. Many mail-order nurseries and garden supply companies also sell window boxes, so be sure to check their catalogues.

INSTALLING WINDOW BOXES

If your windowsill is wide enough, a window box can simply rest upon it. You should anchor the box, though, to make sure it does not slide or blow off the sill. If your windowsill slopes forward, as many do, you may want to place wedges under the front of the box to level it. To securely anchor the box, attach screw eyes to the window box, and corresponding hooks and eyes on the window frame, or attach the eyes to each other with heavy-gauge wire.

If the box projects beyond the edge of the windowsill, attach brackets to the bottom of the box at the front, and screw the other ends into the wall. If necessary, bend the brackets to fit them around the sill. Make sure you use screws that are appropriate for the wall. (Wood screws will not hold in a masonry wall.)

Where windowsills are narrow, it is better to mount window boxes on the wall directly below the window. You can place the brackets either on the bottom of the box or on the back. If you live above the first floor and your window boxes will be viewed from below, you may want to use ornamental brackets of wrought iron or brass.

SUPPORTS FOR CLIMBING PLANTS

Tall plants growing in window boxes, especially in very windy locations, should be supported with dowels or slender stakes. The dowels or stakes can simply be pushed into the soil next to each plant. To avoid damaging the stems, tie the plants loosely to the stakes with soft twine in a figure-eight pattern.

Climbing plants need support, too, and you can use trellises, strings or wires, plastic netting, or pieces of wood lattice. Trellises are generally made of wood, and you will find them in an assortment of configurations, including grids and fan shapes. A trellis is not going to fit inside a window box, of course, but you can mount it on the wall next to the win-

dow if that is where you want to train the vines to grow. Wood lattice and plastic netting can be used the same way. If you do attach a trellis to the wall, put blocks of wood between the trellis and the wall to allow plenty of air to circulate and to provide space for stems and tendrils to twine around the support. Ivy and Virginia creeper will stick to the trellis (or the wall, where their aerial roots can eventually damage bricks or stone) by themselves, but most other vines will need to be fastened to the trellis or guided around strings or wires, at least at first.

A less conspicuous way to support climbers is to train them on strings or wires attached to the back of the window box and to the wall. If you want to train the plants around the window frame, install wires around the frame

and fasten the vines to them at intervals.

TOOLS

Window box gardening requires little in the way of tools. All you will need are a few small hand tools: a cultivator to aerate the soil and scratch in granular fertilizers, a watering can, a hand sprayer for misting and foliar feeding, secateurs or a pruning knife for trimming trees and shrubs and clipping off dead flowers, a small trowel for digging planting holes, and a dibber for planting seeds.

PLANTING

There are two options for putting plants in window boxes. You can plant directly in the boxes, or in individual pots sunk into peat in the boxes. No matter which method you use, be sure every box and liner has drainage holes in the bottom (if your boxes do not have drainage holes you will have to drill them yourself). It is also a good idea to raise the box off the windowsill on wood blocks, so that air can circulate beneath the box. In stone troughs or other containers in which you cannot make drainage holes, put a layer of gravel in the bottom of the box to improve drainage.

Planting directly in the window box is the simplest approach, but having damp soil in constant contact with

the box may damage the window box, especially if it is made of wood or metal. Direct planting also makes it more difficult to remove unhealthy plants (because all the roots intertwine), and to rotate plants in and out of boxes from season to season. However, direct-planting is fine for window boxes that are intended primarily for use in a single season.

Planting in pots allows you to change individual plants quickly, to show off favourite specimens or replace ailing plants. If you move some of your houseplants into outdoor window boxes for the summer, you can slip their pots into the boxes. It is a good idea to surround the pots with peat or sphagnum moss to help conserve moisture and to hide the tops of the pots. When you water the potted plants, dampen the peat or moss around them, too. (The peat or moss should be constantly moist, but not soggy).

Although you have planned your boxes in advance, set the plants on top of the soil before planting to make sure you like the design. Plant window boxes from back to front, putting in the tallest plants first and the shortest ones (or trailers) last. If you are planting one or two small shrubs or trees to serve as focal points, plant them first and then fill in

with the smaller plants. If you are planting some bulbs in a box along with several other plants, plant the bulbs last. If you plant them first you could injure them when you dig holes for the other plants. If you are planting vines, put up the trellises or stakes first, then plant the climbers next to them.

When planting your window boxes, be sure to leave enough space between plants to allow them to grow to their full size. If you crowd plants too close together none of them will grow well. If you are transplanting, dig holes large enough to accommodate all the roots. Set the transplants at the same depth they were growing in their previous pot or tray. Finally, leave the soil level about 2.5 cm (1 in) below the top of each box, to allow room for watering.

Be mindful of the environmental needs of plants in window boxes, just as you would for plants in garden beds and borders. Because there is less soil to insulate them, plants in window boxes are more susceptible to extreme temperatures than plants growing in the ground. Do not set out tender plants too early, before temperatures have warmed up enough, or they may be damaged.

SOIL MIXES

The best soil mixes for plants in window boxes are the same ones that work well for houseplants and outdoor container plants. You can buy packaged soil mixes, called potting composts, or make your own blends. You can use sterilized loam from your garden as a base. Mix the loam with a source of organic matter — compost which you have crumbled into small pieces or pressed through a sieve; peat; or leaf mould. To lighten the texture, add some vermiculite, perlite, or builder's sand. A good all-purpose formula is three parts loam; two parts compost, leaf mould, or peat; and one part vermiculite, perlite, or sand. If you are growing foliage plants, add some well rotted cow manure to provide extra nitrogen. If you are growing flowers, add some bone meal for extra phosphates.

WATERING

Regular watering is essential for plants in window boxes. The small amount of soil in the boxes dries out quickly, especially in hot summer weather. Unless you live in a very rainy climate, you will have to water your window boxes regularly. In hot, dry weather, window boxes need to be watered once or even twice a day.

The best way to judge when plants need water is to stick your finger into the soil; if the soil feels dry 2.5–5 cm (1–2 in) below the surface it is time to water. Do not wait until your plants droop or wilt before watering them. Wilting means that plants are suffering water stress, and although watering may revive them, water-stressed plants grow slowly and produce fewer flowers.

Overwatering creates as many problems for plants as underwatering. When the soil is constantly soggy, plant roots cannot get air (which is essential) and the plants can literally suffocate. Soggy soil also encourages diseases. If your plants develop yellow leaves and drop a lot of leaves, they are probably getting too much water.

When you water your plants, do it gently but thoroughly. Water the soil at the base of the plants; don't just sprinkle the plants from above. Continue watering

until excess water drips from the drainage holes in the bottom of the window box. It is important that the soil be moistened all the way through, so all the roots receive water. Some gardeners like to mist their plants to allow the leaves to absorb moisture directly. If you decide to mist your plants, do so early in the morning or late in the afternoon. Avoid getting water on foliage at midday when the sun is at its hottest (the water droplets act like little lenses, focusing the sunlight and causing

burning of plant leaves). Also avoid misting at night; when foliage remains wet in still night air, fungal diseases may attack it.

If you are going out of town for more than a day, try to get a friend to water your window boxes while you are gone. As a last resort, set the boxes in trays that can hold water to get them by for a day or two.

FERTILIZING

Plants in window boxes will exhaust the nutrients in the soil after about a month. To keep them growing well, you will need to fertilize regularly after the plants are established. Wait until the plants have been growing for several weeks before you feed them; fertilizing young plants too soon overstimulates them, resulting in rapid, weak growth and generally poor performance. Overfeeding plants at any stage of their development will have the same effect.

There are many fertilizers on the market. Granular fertilizers can be sprinkled on the soil surface and gently scratched in with a kitchen fork or small cultivator. When you water the plants, the fertilizer will be dissolved and then absorbed by the roots. Be cautious when applying granular fertilizers because they can burn plant roots if they come in direct contact with them. Apply the fertilizers when soil is moist so that they will dissolve quickly and harmlessly.

Liquid, water-soluble fertilizer is probably the best choice for window box plants. It is easy to use, and its nutrients become available to plants immediately. The fertilizer is diluted with water and then applied to the soil surface or sprayed onto the plants' leaves, a process known as foliar feeding. Foliar feeding produces very quick results, but does not last as long as fertilizer applied to soil, so it should be applied more often.

Both liquid and solid fertilizers are available in various synthetic and organic formulations. Organic gardeners used to have to apply several different materials to get a balanced plant food (such as dried blood for nitrates, bonemeal or rock phosphate for phosphates, wood ash for potash), but in recent years organic fertilizer blends have become available. Good organic liquid fertilizers are fish emulsion and seaweed concentrates. Several brands of powdered organic fertilizers of different nutrient formulations with varying strengths are also available.

When you choose a fertilizer for your window boxes, look for a product that contains balanced amounts of

nitrates, phosphates, and potash, and trace elements as well. Foliage plants grow best with a high-nitrogen fertilizer, such as a 12-4-4 granular product or fish emulsion. Flowering plants prefer more phosphates, such as a 5-10-5 formula.

Feed your plants according to their needs. Fast-growing annuals can be fed with liquid fertilizers every two weeks throughout the growing season, or once a month with granular fertilizers. Perennials vary in their fertilizer requirements. Some,

such as chrysanthemums, need to be fed every two or three weeks; others, such as candytuft, will need far less frequent feedings. Bulbs need no fertilizer at all during their first year until autumn, when a dose of commercial bulb food or bonemeal will nourish them for next year's flowering. Shrubs and trees need fertilizing once or twice a year.

SEASONAL MAINTENANCE

In a garden as small as a window box, grooming is essential. Go over your plants regularly to pick off faded flowers and wilted leaves. Multi-stemmed plants like impatiens need to be pinched back periodically to encourage them to grow bushy and produce lots of flowers. Check climbing plants to make sure they are secured to their supports. Tie up any straggling stems, or nip them off if they are too unruly. Keep shrubs and trees pruned and clipped to maintain a good shape.

Watch closely for signs of pests and diseases. Large pests such as caterpillars, can be picked off the plants by hand and disposed of. Many common pests, such as aphids, whiteflies, and spider mites, can be washed off plants with a hose if the infestation is not too severe. If water does not remove the pests, spray with an insecticide to get rid of them. If your windows are open in summer, chemicals sprayed on your plants will drift into your house, so it is best to use these products with care. Remember to check the undersides of leaves and the leaf axils (where leaves join the stem) as well as the tops of the leaves when looking for pests.

Monitor the plants closely. If you notice any spotted, mildewed, or otherwise unhealthy leaves, pick them off at once. If the symptoms persist, the plant is probably diseased, so pull it up, discard it promptly, and replace it with a new plant. (It is a good idea to grow a few extra plants in the garden or in pots to have substitutes on hand if you need them.)

Prevention is the best strategy for combatting plant diseases, and keeping the garden clean is the best prevention. Keeping weeds pulled and dead leaves and flowers picked off will minimize the chance of infection.

Dwarf trees and shrubs that are kept in window boxes for several years need some special care. You will need to prune their roots as well as their top growth to keep them from outgrowing the box too quickly. Root pruning is done either in early spring or in autumn, when the plants are not in

their most active growth period. If you prune in autumn, do so at least four weeks before you expect the first hard frost, so the root tissues will have time to heal and harden before winter sets in.

Change the soil mix in your window boxes every year. If you are growing

shrubs or perennials that should not be disturbed annually, at least scrape off the top few centimetres (inches) of soil in spring and replace it with fresh soil mix.

PREPARING FOR WINTER
Clean up your window boxes in autumn so they will be ready for planting the following spring. Pull up and discard annuals when the plants stop blooming or are killed by frost. Cut back herbaceous perennials to the soil levels, and prune or trim woody-stemmed perennials, shrubs, and trees. Move tender perennials and houseplants back indoors before the weather turns cold. Isolate plants coming back indoors from the rest of your houseplants for a few weeks to make sure they are not harbouring pests that could spread to other indoor plants. Lift tuberous begonias, dahlias, and other tender tubers and store them indoors over the winter.

If you grew geraniums (pelargoniums) in your window boxes, cut back the plants, pot them up, and bring them indoors for the winter. You might also take cuttings and start new plants indoors. Cut back the plants the following spring to encourage new growth when the plants are moved back to the window boxes.

DIRECTORY OF PLANTS

Actinidia kolomikta · **Kolomikta vine** · Perennial; 5–6.5 m (15–20 ft); climbing. Blooms in late spring; clusters of small white flowers. Leaves are splashed with pink and white. Partial shade or full sun. Not demanding in terms of soil.

Allium schoenoprasum · **Chives** · Perennial; 15–20 cm (6–8 in) tall; upright clumps of grass-like leaves. Bears purple-pink flowers in summer. Full sun to partial shade. Cut onion-flavoured leaves as needed for cooking.

Antirrhinum majus · **Snapdragon** · Grow as annual; compact varieties are 17.5–50 cm (7–20 in) tall; upright. Blooms in summer and again in autumn if faded flower spikes are cut off. Flowers come in red, crimson, scarlet, salmon, pink, yellow, white. Sun or partial shade. Grows best in fairly rich soil, in cool weather.

Arctotis stoechadifolia · **African daisy** · Annual; 25 cm (10 in) tall; upright. Blooms all summer into autumn; large daisy-like flowers in red, rust, orange, apricot, yellow, pink, white. Full sun. Tolerates hot, dry weather.

Aucuba japonica · **Spotted laurel** · Shrub; can reach 3 m (10 ft) if kept outdoors. Also grown as a houseplant.

Smooth, elliptical leaves are spotted and splashed with gold. Partial shade to shade. Move indoors in winter in very cold climates.

Aurinia saxatilis · **Gold dust** · Perennial; 30 cm (12 in) tall; spreading. Blooms in early spring; yellow or gold. Full sun. Grows well in dry soil.

Begonia × semperflorens-cultorum · **Wax begonia, fibrous-rooted begonia** · Annual; 20–30 cm (8–12 in) tall; spreading. Blooms all summer until frost; red, scarlet, rose, pink, white. Does best in partial shade, but will also bloom in full sun or shade. Dependable, sturdy flowers; can also be grown indoors for winter flowers.

Begonia × tuberhybridia · **Tuberous begonia** · Tender bulb; to 35 cm (14 in) tall; upright or cascading, depending upon variety. Blooms from midsummer until frost; large flowers in red, scarlet, orange, salmon, pink, yellow, white. Partial to full shade. For earlier flowers, start tubers indoors a month before last spring frost.

Bellis perennis · **English daisy** · Grow as biennial; 15 cm (6 in) tall; bushy. Blooms in spring and early summer, in red, crimson, pink, white. Partial shade. Does best in cool weather, in moist, well-drained soil.

Beta vulgaris · **Beet, beetroot** · Look for cultivars such as Boltardy that produce small, round roots. Plant in spring. Full sun. Grow best in light soil.

Bletilla striata · **Hardy orchid** · Bulb; 30 cm (12 in) tall; upright. Blooms in early summer; purplish-pink flowers resemble little cattleya orchids. Partial shade. Needs rich, moist but well-drained soil.

Browallia speciosa · Annual; 20–30 cm (8–12 in) tall; bushy. Blooms all summer; violet-blue, lavender, white. Full sun to partial shade. Good plant for front of window boxes.

Buxus sempervirens · **Box** · Hardy evergreen shrub; dwarf varieties grow to 60 cm (2 ft). Small, glossy, aromatic leaves. Full sun to partial shade. Grows slowly; prune to maintain shape.

Caladium species · **Caladium** · Tender bulb; grown for its large, heart-shaped leaves, variegated in green and red, green and pink, green and white. Partial shade to shade. Start tubers indoors a month before last expected spring frost. Lift bulbs in autumn and store indoors over winter.

Calendula officinalis · **Pot marigold** · Annual; 30–45 cm (12–18 in) tall; bushy. Bloom in spring (winter in warm climates); shades of orange, gold, yellow. Full sun. Blooms best in cool weather.

Callistephus chinensis · **China aster** · Annual; 15–60 cm (6–24 in) tall, depending upon variety; upright. Blooms in summer; double flowers in blue-violet, purple, red-violet, rose, pink, white. Full sun.

Catharanthus roseus · **Madagascar periwinkle** · Tender perennial, grow as annual 15–45 cm (6–18 in) tall, depending upon variety; spreading. Blooms from midsummer to frost, in rose, pink, white. Full sun to partial shade. Tolerates a broad range of environmental conditions.

Celosia cristata plumosa · **Prince of Wales feathers** · Annual; 25–60 cm (10–24 in), depending on variety; upright. Blooms from midsummer to frost; soft flower plumes in crimson, scarlet, rose, apricot-orange, bronze, gold, yellow, cream. Full sun. Easy to grow. Good for cutting or drying.

Centaurea Cyanus · **bachelor's button** · Annual; 30 cm–1 m (1–3 ft) tall; upright. Blooms from late spring through summer; blue, pink, maroon, white. Full sun. Plant in autumn for winter flowers in warm climates.

Chamaecyparis species · **False cypress** · Hardy ever-

green tree; dwarf varieties can be grown in window boxes. Upright, conical shape; flat, finely divided leaves. Sun to partial shade.

Cheiranthus species · **Wallflower** · Biennial; 37.5 cm (15 in) tall; upright. Blooms in spring or summer; spikes of fragrant flowers in golden yellow, orange. Full sun. Will bloom the first year from seed.

Chionodoxa species · **Glory-of-the-snow** · Hardy bulb; 10-15 cm (4–6 in) tall; upright. Blooms in early spring; blue flowers with white centers. Full sun to partial shade. Tolerates polluted air.

Chlorophytum comosum · **Spider plant** · Houseplant; long, narrow green or green-and-white striped leaves. Plants periodically send out white flowers on long, drooping stems, which are followed by plantlets that can be removed and potted up. Partial shade. Move indoors for winter.

Chrysanthemum coccineum · **Pyrethum, painted daisy** · Perennial; 60 cm (2 ft) tall; bushy. Blooms in late spring

and early summer; large composite flowers in red, crimson, rose, pink, white. Full sun to partial shade.

Chrysanthemum maximum · **Shasta daisy** · Perennial; compact varieties about 30 cm (12 in) tall; bushy. Blooms in summer; white daisies with yellow centres. Full sun to partial shade. Needs moist, well-drained soil.

Chrysanthemum × *morifolium* · **Garden or hardy chrysanthemum** · Perennial; 30 cm–1 m (1–3 ft) tall, depending upon variety; bushy. Classic autumn flowers in pompon, button, daisy, double, and other forms; many shades of red, orange, bronze, gold, and yellow, also pink, white, and purple. Full sun. Needs rich, well-drained soil and monthly pinching until midsummer to encourage bushiness.

Chrysanthemum ptarmiciflorum · **Dusty miller, silver lace** · Tender perennial; 17.5 cm (7 in) tall; bushy. Grown for its lacy, finely cut, silvery foliage. Full sun. In mild climates, cut back in autumn to encourage bushy plants the next year.

Cineraria maritima · **Dusty miller, silverdust** · Tender perennial; 22.5 cm (9 in) high; bushy. Grown for its silvery, fuzzy foliage. Full sun. In mild climates, cut back in autumn to encourage bushy growth the next year.

Cobaea scandens · **Cup and saucer vine, cathedral bells** · Grow as annual; to 6.5 m (20 ft); climbing. Blooms in summer; bell-shaped flowers are green, turning to violet. Full sun.

Colchicum species · **Autumn crocus** · Hardy bulb; 25–30 cm (10–12 in) tall; upright. Chalice-shaped flowers bloom in autumn, in rose, pink, purple, white. Full sun to partial shade. Easy to grow.

Coleus blumei · Grow as annual; 20–37.5 cm (8–15 in) tall; bushy (cascading variety is also available). Blooms in summer, but grown for its variegated foliage in various combinations of deep red, red-brown, pink, dark green, lime green, and white. Sun or shade. Can be grown indoors as a winter houseplant from cuttings or seeds started in late summer.

Cordyline terminalis · **Ti plant** · Houseplant; 30–60 cm (1–2 ft) tall; upright plants with narrow green leaves striped and splashed with pink and cream. Partial shade. Grows best in well-drained soil. Bring indoors for winter.

Cosmos bipinnatus · **Cosmos** · Annual; 60 cm–1 m (2–3 ft) tall; upright. Blooms in summer, in yellow, orange, red, rose, pink, white. Full sun. Tolerates poor soil.

Crocus species · **Crocus** · Hardy bulb; 7.5–15 cm (3–6 in) tall; upright. Blooms in early spring or autumn, de-pending upon species or variety, in purple, lavender, gold, white, white striped with purple. Spring-blooming types grow in full sun to partial shade; autumn crocus does best in full sun. Very easy to grow.

Dahlia species · **Dahlia** · Tender bulb (tuberous-rooted); dwarf types can be grown from seed and bloom first year. Dwarf varieties are 30–60 cm (1–2 ft) tall; bushy. Blooms from late summer until frost; shades of yellow, orange, red, crimson, pink, white. Full sun. Lift and store roots over winter in all but frost-free climates.

Daucus sativa · **Carrot** · For window boxes choose a small-rooted variety such as 'Early Nantes'. Full sun. Grows best in sandy soil.

Dianthus species · **Annual garden pinks** · Annual; 15–20 cm (6–8 in) tall; bushy. Blooms in summer, in scarlet, red, crimson, coral, salmon, pink, white. Full sun. Tolerates polluted air.

Dianthus species · **Perennial garden pinks** · Perennial; 20–35 cm (8–14 in) tall;

spreading. Blooms in spring, in coral, salmon, pink, white. Fringed flowers are clove-scented. Full sun. Easy to grow and tolerant of many types of soil. Tolerates polluted air.

Dianthus barbatus · **Sweet William** · Biennial; 15–45 cm (6–18 in) tall; upright. Blooms in late spring to early summer; clusters of flowers in shades of red, rose, pink, white, many striped with a darker or lighter shade. Full sun.

Dimorphotheca sinuata · **Cape marigold** · Tender perennial, usually grown as annual; 30 cm (12 in) tall; upright. Blooms all summer until frost; shades of yellow, orange, apricot, salmon, white, with dark centre. Full sun. Does well in dry climates; needs well-drained soil.

Eschscholzia californica · **California poppy** · Annual; 20–30 cm (10–12 in) tall; spreading. Blooms in summer; yellow-orange. Full sun. Grows best in cool weather.

Euonymus fortunei · **Wintercreeper** · Shrub; trailing or climbing. Grown for its evergreen variegated foliage. Full sun to partial shade. Tolerates polluted air.

Euphorbia marginata · **Snow-on-the-mountain** · Annual; 45 cm (18 in) tall; bushy. Grown for its white-edged green leaves. Full sun to partial shade. Does well in poor soil and in hot, dry climates.

Fatsia japonica · Shrub, grown as a houseplant; 1.5 m (5 ft). Woody stems with large, glossy, lobed leaves. Partial shade. Grows best in cool temperatures, in moist soil. Prune back in spring.

Galanthus nivalis · **Snowdrop** · Hardy bulb; 10–15 cm (4–6 in) tall; upright. Blooms in early spring; nodding white flowers. Partial shade.

Gazania species · **Treasure flower** · Perennial, often grown as annual; 20–30 cm (8–12 in) tall, depending on variety; upright. Blooms in summer until frost; large, daisylike flowers in red, orange, yellow, rose, and bicolors. Full sun.

Gerbera jamesonii · **Transvaal daisy** · Tender perennial, often grown as annual; 30–60 cm (1–2 ft) tall; upright. Blooms in summer; daisylike flowers in shades of red, scarlet, crimson, orange, pink, yellow, white. Full sun to partial shade.

Gladiolus species · **Gladiolus** · Tender bulb; miniature varieties are 45–60 cm (18–24 in) tall; upright. Blooms in summer; spikes of red, crimson, scarlet, orange, coral, salmon, yellow, white. Full sun. Lift bulbs in autumn and store indoors over winter.

Gomphrena globosa · **Globe amaranth** · Annual; 45–60 cm (18–24 in) upright. Blooms in summer; ball-like flowers in purple, magenta, rose, pink, and white. Full

sun. Flowers dry well.

Hedera helix · **Ivy** · Perennial; trailing or climbing. Grown for its foliage, available in several species with differently variegated leaves. Grows in partial shade, shade, or sun. Tolerates polluted air.

Heliotropium arborescens · **Heliotrope** · Perennial, usually grown as annual; 37.5 cm (15 in) tall; bushy. Blooms in summer; clusters of fragrant blue-violet flowers. Full sun. Grows well in any good soil.

Hosta species · **Plantain lily** · Perennial; 30–60 cm (12–24 in) high; spreading clumps of upright leaves. Blooms in late summer, but more valuable for its foliage, which comes in different combinations of green and white or green and gold. Grows in sun or shade.

Hyacinthus orientalis · **Hyacinth** · Hardy bulb; about 25 cm (10 in) tall; upright. Blooms in spring, sweetly fragrant flowers in blue, violet, pink, red, yellow, white. Full sun to partial shade. Grows best in well-drained soil.

Iberis sempervirens · **Perennial candytuft** · Perennial; to 25 cm (10 in) tall; spreading. Blooms in spring; lacy heads of white flowers. Full sun. Does well in dry soil. Tolerates polluted air.

Iberis umbellata · **Annual candytuft** · Annual; 20–25 cm (8–10 in) tall; upright.

Blooms lavishly all summer in purple, lavender, carmine, rose, pink, or white. Full sun. Dependable and easy to grow; often self-seeds. Tolerates polluted air.

Impatiens balsamina · **Balsam** · Annual; 25–75 cm (10–30 in) tall, depending upon variety; upright. Blooms from summer until frost; red, scarlet, salmon, pink, mauve, purple, white. Full sun. Does best in rich, moist but well-drained soil.

Impatiens species · **Impatiens** · Tender perennial, usually grown as annual; 10–45 cm (4–18 in) tall; bushy. Blooms all summer, in shades of red, rose, pink, orange, salmon, white. Partial to full shade. Pinch the plants to make them bushy and keep them producing lots of flowers.

Ipomea alba · **Moonflower** · Tender perennial, grown as annual to 4.5 m (15 ft); climbing. Blooms in summer; large, fragrant white flowers resembling morning glories open at night.

Ipomoea purpurea · **Morning glory** · Annual; to 2.4 m (8 ft); climbing. Blooms all summer, in blue, lavender, violet, red, pink, white. Full sun. Easy to grow in average soil.

Juniperus species · **Juniper** · Evergreen trees; dwarf varieties grow from 45 cm–1.5 m (1½–5 ft) tall. Columnar, pyramidal, or spreading, depending upon variety; small, needle-like leaves. Full sun to partial shade. Prune to maintain neat shape.

Lactuca sativa · **Lettuce** · Butterhead, looseleaf, and a small Cos cultivar ('Little Gem') are best for window boxes. Sow seeds in early spring; grows best in cool weather. Full sun to partial shade.

Lathyrus odoratus · **Sweet pea** · Annual; climbing. Blooms in spring and summer; fragrant flowers in red, scarlet, rose, pink, lavender, purple, white. Full sun. Grows best in cool weather.

Lobelia erinus · Annual; to 15 cm (6 in) tall, or cascading; bushy. Dainty plants are covered with small flowers all summer until frost; in blue, blue-violet, rosy red, rose, white. Full sun to partial shade. Easy to grow and good for the front of a window box.

Lobularia maritima · **Sweet alyssum** · Annual; 10–15 cm (4–6 in) tall; spreading. Blooms from spring to frost; small, fragrant flowers in white, purple, rose. Full sun to partial shade. Use in front of window boxes. Tolerates polluted air.

Lycopersicon lycopersicum · **Tomato** · Dwarf varieties grow only 37.5–50 cm (15–20 in) tall. Bushy plants. Full sun.

Matthiola incana · **Stocks** · Annual; 30–45 cm (12-18 in) tall; upright. Spikes of fragrant flowers bloom in summer; in crimson, rose, pink, lavender, blue, purple, yellow, white. Full sun. Grows best in cool weather.

Muscari species · **Grape hyacinth** · Hardy bulb; 15–25 cm (6–10 in) tall; upright. Spikes of fragrant, tiny, bell-shaped flowers appear in spring, in blue or white. Full sun to partial shade.

Myosotis sylvatica · **Garden forget-me-not** · Biennial; 30 cm (12 in) tall; spreading. Blooms in spring or early summer; clusters of little, mid-blue flowers. Partial shade. Plants may self-sow.

Narcissus species · **Daffodil and narcissus** · Hardy bulb; 15–50 cm (6–20 in) tall, depending upon variety; upright. Blooms in early spring, in shades of yellow, cream, white (some varieties have central cups of orange or salmon). Full sun to partial shade.

Nepeta species · **Catmint** · Perennial; 30 cm (12 in) tall; upright flowers on spreading plants. Blooms from spring to autumn, in lavender-blue spikes. Full sun to partial shade. Keep faded flowers picked off to prolong bloom. Foliage is aromatic.

Nicotiana species · **Tobacco plant** · Tender perennial, usually grown as annual; to 45 cm (18 in) tall; bushy. Blooms all summer, in red, rose, pink, white, lime green. Full sun to partial shade. Some varieties are fragrant.

Nierembergia hippomanica · **Cup flower** · Perennial, often grown as annual; 15 cm (6 in) high; spreading. Blooms in summer and autumn in violet-blue. Full sun to partial shade.

Nigella damascena · **Love-in-a-mist** · Annual; 45 cm (18 in) tall; upright. Blooms in summer, in red, pink, purple, white. Full sun. The unusual seed pods can be dried and used in arrangements.

Ocimum Basilicum · **Basil** · Annual; 25–60 cm (10–24 in) tall, depending on variety. Foliage comes in varying sizes, some ruffled, some purple, others lemon or cinnamon scented. Full sun to partial shade. Pinch back plants to encourage bushiness. Can be used fresh or dried.

Papaver nudicaule · **Iceland poppy** · Perennial; 40 cm (16 in) tall; upright. Blooms in spring; in scarlet, red, rose, pink, orange, yellow, cream. Full sun. Will bloom first year from seed if sown early.

Papaver Rhoeas · **Field poppy, Shirley poppy** · Annual; 45 cm (18 in) tall; upright. Blooms in summer; in red, orange, salmon, apricot, pink. Full sun. Sow directly in window box; does not transplant well.

Pelargonium × hortorum · **Zonal geranium** · Tender perennial; 25–45 cm (10–18 in) tall; upright. Blooms in summer; shades of red, salmon, pink, rose, white. Full sun. Best in well-drained soil. Bring indoors or take cuttings in autumn to keep plants growing over winter. Pinch plants often to encourage bushy shape.

Pelargonium peltatum · **Ivy-leaved geranium** · Tender perennial, usually grown as annual; cascading, bushy. Blooms in summer; shades of red, rose, pink, lavender, purple, white. Full sun.

Petroselinum crispum · **Parsley** · Biennial; about 30 cm (12 in) tall. Leaves are curly and finely cut or flat and deeply cut, depending upon variety. Full sun to partial shade. May self-sow.

Petunia × hybrida · **Petunia** · Annual; about 30 cm (12 in) tall; spreading. Blooms from early summer until frost; single or double flowers, some ruffled or fringed, in shades of red, rose, pink, salmon, yellow, purple, white; also various striped combinations. Full sun. Keep faded flowers picked off to promote continued lavish bloom. Grandiflora hybrids bear larger, flashier flowers than Multiflora hybrids; Multifloras hold up in rain and wind.

Peucedanum graveolens · **Dill** · Annual; to 1 m (3 ft) tall; upright. Feathery foliage; blooms in summer, flat yellow-green flower heads. Full sun.

Phlox Drummondii · **Annual phlox** · Annual; 17.5–45 cm

(7–15 in) tall; bushy. Blooms all summer; shades of red, rose, pink, lavender, white. Full sun. Grows best in rich soil.

Portulaca grandiflora · **Sun plant** · Annual; 15 cm (6 in) tall; spreading. Blooms in summer; in red, magenta, rose, pink, salmon, orange, yellow, white. Full sun. Does well in hot, dry climates.

Primula × polyantha · **Polyanthus primrose** · Perennial; 15–20 cm (6–8 in) tall; upright. Blooms in spring in red, rose, pink, purple, blue, yellow, white, with bright yellow centre. Partial shade. Needs acid soil. Tolerates polluted air.

Rosa hybrids · **Miniature rose** · Shrub; 25–37.5 cm (10–15 in) tall; bushy. Blooms in summer; shades of red, rose, pink, salmon, orange, yellow, white. Full sun. Needs well-drained soil. In cold climates, provide winter protection or move plants indoors.

Salvia farinacea · **Mealycup sage** · Tender perennial, often grown as annual; 45 cm (18 in) tall; upright. Blooms

in summer; spikes of violet-blue flowers. Full sun.

Salvia splendens · **Scarlet sage** · Grown as annual; dwarf varieties are about 25 cm (10 in) tall; upright. Blooms in summer; spikes of brilliant red flowers. Full sun.

Scilla siberica · **Siberian squill** · Hardy bulb; 10–15 cm (4–6 in) tall; upright. Deep blue flowers bloom in early spring. Full sun to partial shade. Very easy to grow.

Sedum acre · **Biting stonecrop** · Perennial; 5–12.5 cm (2–5 in) tall; creeping. Blooms in late spring; clusters of small yellow flowers; succulent light green leaves. Full sun. Does well in dry soil.

Sedum sieboldii · Perennial; 15–22.5 cm (6–9 in) tall; spreading. Blooms in late summer to early autumn; clusters of pink flowers; succulent grey-green leaves with red edges. Full sun. Does well in dry soil.

Sedum spurium · Perennial; 15 cm (6 in) tall; creeping. Blooms in summer; clusters of bright red flowers; succulent green leaves tinged with red. Full sun. Does well in dry soil.

Tagetes patula · **French marigold** · Annual; 15–25 cm (6–10 in) tall, depending upon variety; bushy. Blooms all summer until frost; shades of yellow, orange, mahogany-red. Full sun.

Thunbergia alata · **Black-**

eyed Susan · Grown as annual; to 1.5 m (5 ft); climbing. Blooms in summer; in orange, golden yellow, white, with dark centre. Full sun. Can be trained on a trellis.

Thymus vulgaris · **Thyme** · Perennial; 15–30 cm (6–12 in) tall; creeping. Blooms in summer; tiny pink or white flowers. Small leaves can be lemon-scented or variegated in some varieties. Full sun.

Torenia Fournieri · **Wishbone flower** · Annual; 20 cm (8 in) tall; bushy. Blooms in summer; lavender flowers have deep purple markings and a yellow spot. Full sun to partial shade.

Trachymene coerulea · **Blue lace flower** · Annual; 75 cm (30 in) tall; upright. Blooms in summer; lavender-blue flower heads similar to Queen Anne's lace. Full sun.

Tropaeolum peregrinum · **Canary creeper** · Grown as annual; to 2.4 m (8 ft); climbing. Blooms in summer; bright yellow flowers similar to nasturtiums. Full sun to partial shade.

Tropaeolum species · **Nasturtium** · Annual; compact varieties cascade or grow to 30 cm (12 in) tall; climbing varieties reach 1.8 m (6 ft). Blooms in summer; shades of red, mahogany, orange, golden yellow. Full sun. Needs average, well-drained soil; plants produce fewer flowers in rich soil. Both flowers and leaves are edible.

Tulipa species · **Tulip** · Hardy bulb. Kaufmanniana and Greigii hybrids grow 12.5–30 cm (5–12 in) tall; various species tulips grow about 15 cm (6 in) tall. Bloom in spring; shades of red, orange, apricot, pink, yellow, white. Full sun to partial shade.

Verbena × hybrida · **Garden verbena** · Grow as annual; 20–25 cm (8–10 in) tall; bushy. Blooms in summer; maroon, red, scarlet, rose, pink, salmon, purple, white. Full sun. Does well in poor soil; can withstand hot weather.

Veronica species · **Speedwell** · Perennial; compact varieties about 37.5 cm (15 in) tall; upright. Blooms in mid- to late summer; spikes of blue or rosy pink flowers. Full sun. Needs moist soil.

Vinca minor · **Periwinkle** · Perennial; 10-15 cm (4–6 in) tall; trailing. Blooms in spring and early summer; blue flowers. Grows in either sun or shade. Leaves stay green all winter.

Viola cornuta · **Horned vio-**

let, tufted pansy · Perennial; 15 cm (6 in) tall; bushy. Blooms from spring to frost; in purple, blue, orange, gold, white. Partial shade. Blooms first year from seed if sown early. In warm climates, plant in autumn for winter flowers. Grows best in rich soil.

Viola odorata · **Violet** · Perennial; 10–15 cm (4–6 in) tall; spreading. Blooms in spring; dainty flowers of purple, blue-violet, or white above heart-shaped leaves. Partial shade. Best in moist soil.

Viola tricolor var. *hortensis* · **Heartsease** · Perennial; to 30 cm (12 in) tall; spreading. Blooms in summer; tricoloured flowers of lavender, yellow, and violet. Full sun to partial shade.

Viola × wittrockiana · **Pansy** · Biennial, often grown as annual; 15–17.5 cm (6–7 in) tall; bushy. Blooms in spring; burgundy, deep red, orange, yellow, rose, purple, violet, blue, white, with or without "faces." Full sun to partial shade. Needs rich, well-drained soil; does best in cool weather. In warm climates, can be planted in fall for winter flowers.

Zinnia species · **Zinnia** · Annual; dwarf varieties are 15–30 cm (6–12 in) tall; upright. Daisylike single or double flowers bloom in summer; in red, scarlet, pink, orange, yellow, white. Full sun. Tolerates hot, dry weather; may develop mildew in cool, damp climates.

ACKNOWLEDGMENTS

Special thanks to those who have
made this book as much of a
pleasure to create as we hope it is
to behold: John Blezard, Lesley
Ehlers, Marta Hallett, Caroline
Herter, Sarah Kirshner, Ellen
Milionis, Klaasje Mull and
Pam Thomas.